TYRELL BENTLEY

CRYPTOCURRENCY MINING

The Ultimate Guide to Cryptocurrency and Bitcoin Mining, Learn the Inner Workings of How Bitcoin Mining Works and How to Gain Massive Profits

Descrierea CIP a Bibliotecii Naţionale a României
TYRELL BENTLEY
    CRYPTOCURRENCY MINING. The Ultimate Guide to Cryptocurrency and Bitcoin Mining, Learn the Inner Workings of How Bitcoin Mining Works and How to Gain Massive Profits / Tyrell Bentley – Bucharest: Editura My Ebook, 2021
    ISBN

TYRELL BENTLEY

CRYPTOCURRENCY MINING

The Ultimate Guide to Cryptocurrency and Bitcoin Mining, Learn the Inner Workings of How Bitcoin Mining Works and How to Gain Massive Profits

My Ebook Publishing House
Bucharest, 2021

TABLE OF CONTENTS

INTRODUCTION

It is no longer news that the adoption of digital currencies as a means of making payment is rapidly gaining momentum around the world. Bitcoin, which is the first example of the growing category of money known as the cryptocurrency, is the most popular and widely accepted of them all.

Bitcoin is a peer-to-peer electronic cash system that was invented by a software developer called Satoshi Nakamoto, and it is currently taking the lead amongst other digital currencies. It is an electronic payment system based on mathematical proof that is created and held electronically. Bitcoin is also a decentralized form of cryptocurrency that is independent of any central authority – meaning, there is no single institution controlling the Bitcoin network.

This eBook is going to help you go beyond a basic understanding of Bitcoin and the mining of it. When you are finished reading, you'll be ready to get started mining Bitcoins today!

What is Bitcoin Mining?

In traditional fiat currency systems, money is printed by the government and released into circulation whenever it is needed. Bitcoins, on the other hand, aren't printed, rather they are mined. Computers around the world 'mine' for coins by competing with each other using software that solves mathematical problems.

Bitcoin is mined by people, and increasingly, businesses using computing power in a distributed network. It can be transferred electronically and costs very little in transaction fees. The first groups of people to stake their claim in Bitcoin mining were cypherpunks, cryptographers, technically-minded libertarians and multi-talented hackers.

Miners get rewarded in Bitcoins for each new block that they discover and for every transaction that gets finalized. Bitcoin mining usually involves two main aspects; these are:

confirming transactions to the blockchain and introducing new Bitcoins to the system.

The blockchain is normally kept in a chronological order to provide the proof needed to complete transactions. Hence, it makes it extremely difficult and nearly impossible to undo transactions because it will require new proof on not just one block, but on all the others.

The network is programmed in such a way that when two blocks (or pending transactions) are found simultaneously, the entire Bitcoin network works on the first block they've found. It follows a one-block-at- a-time process so that no new block is solved until the penultimate block has been finalized. Then, whoever solves the block gets rewarded with Bitcoins.

The process of solving subsequent blocks continues on to the next block, and it keeps going on and on in circles with a reward for each successful block that gets finalized.

As the mining population increases in the field, there is a proportionate increase in the difficulty of finding new blocks. This difficulty is enhanced because the network is always wanting to ensure that the average time for miners to find a block is limited to 10 minutes. Hence, there is an inherent cutthroat competition lingering among the miners because they only have 10 minutes to finalize their transactions. With this rule actively in place, no one person can control the blockchain, rather, a series of miners get to finalize transactions.

Bitcoin Mining Terminology

To begin your journey into Bitcoin mining, you will need to run software with specialized hardware. We will go into further details about this in the next few chapters. But first, we are going to explain how Bitcoin mining works by defining the basic technical terms that are commonly used in mining. These terms include:

Block:

A block is a group of Bitcoin transactions that are collected during a set period from current pending transactions. These transactions are usually entered into an ever-growing list of blocks, also known as the blockchain, by the miner. It is clearly visible to everyone who is a part of the Bitcoin network. It is estimated that a new block is created on average every ten minutes.

Proof of Work Hashing:

This is the function which miners perform to define a new block. It is usually done to ensure that the Bitcoin blockchain is functioning properly. Miners compete with each other to solve a cryptographic "puzzle," known as a hash, by using raw computational power. When a miner correctly hashes the current block, he successfully solves the "puzzle," thus proving his investment of work. He is then rewarded with a certain number of newly-created Bitcoins.

Block Reward:

This refers to the number of newly-created Bitcoins. Bitcoins usually undergoes a halving process every four years (or every 210,000 blocks). As first, the number was set to 50, then it was halved to 25 in late-2012, and 12.5 in mid-2016. It is the only way in which new Bitcoins can be created by miners following the code's rate and limit. This process is expected to continue until all Bitcoins are created.

Hashrate:

This is the measure of a miner's computational power. It is the number of hashes per the amount of time it took to solve them. The higher a miner's relative power is, the more solutions he is likely to find, thus earning more Bitcoins for himself. The unit of measurement of hashrate was initially in hash per second H/s), due to the increasing speed of mining hardware. However, H/s eventually began having prefixes with SI units which consists of the following:

- Kilohash = KH/s (thousands of H/s), then
- Megahash = MH/s (millions of H/s), then
- Gigahash = GH/s (billions of H/s), then
- Terahash = TH/s (trillions of H/s), and finally
- Petahash = PH/s (quadrillions of H/s).

The increase in hashrate would naturally make one conclude that it would be much easier and faster for blocks to be found by miners. However, as earlier pointed out, it takes roughly 10 minutes for new blocks to be found. It is this difficulty measure which is automatically adjusted every two weeks that prevent the blocks from being found easily. The difficulty measure rises and falls accordingly, in response to the total hashrate.

BTC/XBT exchange rate:

This is the current fiat price of Bitcoin. It is highly important for calculating profitability.

W/xHash/s:

This means Watts per hashrate per second. The mining of Bitcoin takes into consideration the amount of electricity consumed. Therefore, the price paid per Watt will greatly influence profitability.

Mining Pool:

A mining pool is a group of miners who come together in agreement to share block rewards in proportion to their contributed mining power. As a sole miner, unless you command a tremendous hashrate, you may find it difficult to solve a block on your own. Aside from that, mining alone is not always profitable now because of the amount spent on hardware and electricity.

By joining forces with other miners in a so-called pool, you stand a better chance of solving a block with the advantage of the pool's total hashrate which means earning more profits than when you mine alone. Whenever a block is solved successfully, the pool rewards each miner according to the amount of their contributed hashrate (fewer commissions and the likes). Joining a top mining pool will help you earn Bitcoins even faster.

Why Do People Mine Bitcoin?

There are several reasons why people mine Bitcoin. Mining is the only way Bitcoin is produced. Also, unlike conventional currency which is based on gold and silver, Bitcoin is based on mathematics.

People around the world use software programs that follow a mathematical formula to produce Bitcoins. The beauty of this is that the mathematical formula is freely available, so basically, anyone can check it. Also, the mining software is open source, so anyone can look it up to verify that the inputs correspond to the desired outputs.

People want the freedom that the mining of Bitcoins provides, and the benefits that come with it. The reasons why they mine Bitcoins can be summarized by the characteristics of Bitcoin itself. These characteristics are practically absent or inconsistent in the conventional government- backed currencies listed as follows:

1. It is decentralized

This is one of the major reasons why people mine Bitcoins, and that is because the Bitcoin network is not controlled by one central authority. Conventional currency's central banks can just decide to take people's money away from them, like was experienced in Cyprus in early 2013 by the Central European Bank. With Bitcoins, every machine involved in its mining forms part of a large network, and they all work together, although competitively. Also, even if some part of the network abruptly goes offline for some reason, the money keeps on flowing nonetheless.

2. It is easily set up

Getting started with mining Bitcoins is a relatively faster and easier process compared to conventional banks. With Bitcoin mining, you get your Bitcoin address in seconds, with no hassle and no fees payable.

Unfortunately, the same cannot be said of conventional banks which make you jump through hoops simply to open a bank account. Not to mention the herculean task and bureaucracy synonymous with setting up a merchant bank account.

3. It is completely transparent

Another reason why people mine Bitcoins is because of its transparency. You can access details of every single transaction that has ever been made on the Bitcoin network via a large version of a general ledger known as the Blockchain. You can also confirm the total amount of Bitcoins stored in a publicly-used Bitcoin address, though the identity of the owner of the address remains anonymous. For those who want to make their activities even more opaque on the Bitcoin network, they can do so by making use of different Bitcoin addresses and by not transferring large amounts of Bitcoin to a single address.

4. Minimal transaction fees

Unlike conventional bank systems that charge high fees on international money transfers, mining of Bitcoins eliminates going through the middleman; you get to enjoy very minute transaction fees.

5. It is fast

Nothing beats the speed of a Bitcoin transaction. You can send money from any part of the world to another, and it will arrive in the recipient's Blockchain wallet in minutes, as soon as the Bitcoin network processes the payment.

6. It is non-retrievable

Once a transfer has been completed, and the Bitcoins are sent, there is no possibility of retrieving them back. This is because it requires the proofs for all of the transactions before the one you want to reverse. The Bitcoins you send out are gone forever and can only be reversed if the recipient agrees to send them back. It is therefore very important that you are sure that you really want a transaction before going ahead with it.

7. It is secure

The mining of Bitcoins allows individuals to become architects of their own wealth but also prevents any one person from gaining enough power to block transactions. This is seen as an advantage and another reason why people mine Bitcoins because of the security of its transactions. It is an ingenious means of payment that effectively ensures that the risk of fraudulent activities being perpetrated is significantly curbed.

Getting Started Mining

To get started as a major Bitcoin miner, there are two specific things that you'll need. Aside from having cheaper electricity, you will need access to the latest mining hardware. Since the second halving event that took place in early July 2016, the mining of Bitcoins has become even tougher, with the reward for successfully mining a block dropping from 25 Bitcoins down to 12.5.

Also, with the Chinese taking the lead in the Bitcoin mining game, you'll need to work with the best available miners to be able to compete.

However, before we delve into the Bitcoin hardware you will need, you must first gain an understanding of a few technical terms.

Hashrate

As earlier explained, the hashrate refers to the measure of how many attempts at solving a Bitcoin block a miner tries per second. The more attempts, the more chances the miner has of solving the block and claiming the 12.5 Bitcoin reward.

Joule per Gigahash (J/GH)

A joule is a unit for measuring energy, and it represents one watt over one second. Electricity is a major recurring expense for miners, and therefore the joule per gigahash (J/GH) is especially important when making comparisons between miners. It is estimated that the electrical efficiency of an Application-specific integrated circuit (ASIC) miner is expected to go higher in indirect proportion to the fewer joules used to produce a Gigahash.

Difficulty

When the term difficulty is used in Bitcoin mining hardware, it simply refers to an automatic control measure that prevents Bitcoin blocks from being solved increasingly quickly.

The difficulty level of mining adjusts to the current hashrate, ensuring the blocks are solved every 10 minutes on average.

Profitability

This refers to a bottom-line number from calculating the current Bitcoin price and Difficulty, including your miner's cost and hashrate and your electrical cost in fiat money per kWh. The Difficulty mechanism, which adjusts itself quite frequently, together with the volatile price of Bitcoin, creates uncertainty about the future profitability of Bitcoin mining.

However, using an online mining profitability calculator can prove very useful for this purpose. You should also create a custom spreadsheet containing inputs showing various exchange rate and Difficulty projections. Also, ensure that you take into consideration probable downtime due to software or hardware failures, power cuts, and the like.

Break-even point

This refers to the duration taken for your miner hardware to pay for itself.

Pool Fees

As mentioned earlier, mining pools are cooperative groups of miners who pull together to improve their hash-power. They distribute any rewards the pool earns in accordance with each individual miner's hashrates.

There are various types of pools, and each has their unique fees and reward structures. The larger the pool, the more frequent returns can be expected, though often, the higher the fees.

Top Hardware for Bitcoin Mining

Now that we have acquired a basic understanding of the metrics used to assess Bitcoin mining hardware, we will now identify the various mining hardware that is currently in use. They include the following:

Bitmain's AntMiner S9

The AntMiner S9 is manufactured by Bitmain – the current leading manufacturer of publically-available ASIC hardware. It is the ideal Bitcoin mining hardware for mining-for-profit on a small scale. It comes with a hashrate of 11.8 – 14 TH/s (figures are approximate and may vary by 5%), it consumes 1350 Watts of electricity (figures are approximate and may vary by 10%), and possesses a power efficiency of 0.1 Joule per GH (figures are approximate and may vary by 10%).

It has a built-in controller, produces 70dB noise at 4ft/1.2m (figures are approximate and may vary by 10%), and it has a chip process of 16nm. A brand new S9 currently costs between $1831 to $2016 less shipping fees (figures are approximate and may vary by 10%).

Its profitability is plausible (assuming an electricity cost of 10c (US) per kW/h, a 2.5% pool fee and at the current Bitcoin price), and it has a break-even point of 0.9 years, as per CoinWarz's calculator, assuming an electricity cost of 10c (US) per kW/h and a 2.5% pool fee at the current Bitcoin price.

The S9 is the latest model of hardware from Bitmain, and it is the first ASIC to market with a 16 Nanometer (nm) semiconductor fabrication process. This means that the circuits in the S9 BM1387 are approximately half the size of previous generation mining chips.

The S9 is fully capable of running on a standard Power Supply Unit, (PSU) better known as a computer, but it is often recommended that you use Antminer's APW3-12-1600-B2. It is high-quality hardware that is extremely power-efficient and designed specifically for mining.

Bitmain's AntMiner S7

The AntMiner S7 is also a product of Bitmain, and it is the most popular of all the Bitcoin mining hardware. You can readily find the S7 in any major mining operation, and it also has a very good second-hand value. It comes with a hashrate of 4.73 TH/s (figures are approximate and may vary by 5%), it consumes 1350 Watts of electricity (figures are approximate and may vary by 10%), and possesses a power efficiency of 0.25 Joule per GH (figures are approximate and may vary by 10%).

It also has a built-in controller, produces 62dB noise at 4ft/1.2m (figures are approximate and may vary by 10%), and it has a chip process of 28nm. A brand new S7 currently goes for $440 less shipping fees, while a second- hand S7 costs around $440 to $674 (figures are approximate and may vary by 10%).

It has a marginal profitability (assuming an electricity cost of 10c (US) per kW/h, a 2.5% pool fee and at the current Bitcoin price), and reaches a break-even point of 2.6 years, as per CoinWarz's calculator, assuming an electricity cost of 10c (US) per kW/h and a 2.5% pool fee at the current Bitcoin price.

The S7 is loved for its affordable price tag among other things, which make it an easy introduction model for prospective miners. It provides a maximum efficiency that can be extracted from a 28nm process and has room for further improvement through skilled modification.

It is great hardware for use in experimenting with alternative energy solutions or software and hardware modifications. It is a high-quality performer that can also turn a profit. It is also available as a variant model – the S7-LN model, which comes with a built-in 700W power supply. It is cheaper, uses less power and is suitable for home and office use.

Canaan's Avalon6

A lot of people are unhappy about Bitmain's dominance of the Bitcoin mining hardware market. Given the fact that Bitmain controls 18% of the network hashrate in the form of AntPool, it is easy to see why such concerns arise.

Unfortunately, there is currently a shortage of suitable alternative hardware. The Avalon6 from Canaan Creative, however, is the only best possible alternative to Bitmain's hardware. It is very good hardware that uses about 300W less power than the AntMiner S7 from Bitmain.

It comes with a hashrate of 3.5 TH/s (figures are approximate and may vary by 5%), it consumes 1050 Watts of electricity (figures are approximate and may vary by 10%), and possesses a power efficiency of 0.29 Joule per GH (figures are approximate and may vary by 10%).

The Avalon6 also has a separate controller, produces 55dB noise at 4ft/ 1.2m (figures are approximate and may vary by 10%), and it has a chip process of 28nm. Without a built-in controller, the Avalon6 will need to be run from a Raspberry Pi (B, B+ or RPi2). The best part about this is that a single RasPi can run up to 50 units.

A brand new Avalon6 currently goes for $550 less shipping fees, while a second-hand Avalon6 costs around $360 to $875 (figures are approximate and may vary by 10%). It has a possible profitability (assuming an electricity cost of 10c (US) per kW/h, a 2.5% pool fee and at the current Bitcoin price), and its break-even point peaks at 7 years, as per CoinWarz's calculator, assuming an electricity cost of 10c (US) per kW/h and a 2.5% pool fee at the current Bitcoin price.

What software is needed?

Bitcoin mining software is somewhat of the 'middle-man' between the hardware, and the users and the Blockchain network. They help the mining hardware by transmitting super calculations performed by the hardware on which they are installed to the Blockchain network.

The mining software is also essential for monitoring the performance of the hardware on which they are installed. The software monitor activities like the hashrate, average speed, and the fan speed of the mining hardware.

Below are some of the best Bitcoin mining software available today. They were chosen based on their running environment and operating system.

Bitcoin Miner

The Bitcoin miner software is especially renowned for its profit calculation feature. This feature provides details of your mining status as to whether you're gaining profits or running at a loss. The software also has an easy to use interface. It is able to switch to power saving mode, it supports fast share submissions and is available for Windows and MacOS X Operating environments.

BTCMiner

The BTCMiner is an open source Bitcoin Miner that is manufactured for the ZTEX USB-FPGA modules 1.5 boards. Its boards come with USB ports that are great for programming and communication. The BTCMiner is available for Windows and MacOS X Operating environments.

CGMiner

The CGMiner is reputably the most commonly used of all the Bitcoin miners. It owes its popularity to its super features which comprise of fan speed control, remote interface capabilities, self-detection of new blocks, multi GPU support, and much more. The CGMiner is available for Windows, Mac OS X, and Linux platforms.

BFGMiner

The BFGMiner bears some similarities with the CGMiner, but one particular feature sets it apart, and that is the fact that it was designed specifically for ASICs and not Graphics Processing Units (GPU). The BFGMiner is available for the Windows, Mac OS X, and Linux platforms.

EasyMiner

Finally, we have the EasyMiner. The EasyMiner is a GUI based software that acts as a wrapper for CG and BFG miner software. It can be used for both solo and pool mining operations. Another super feature of the EasyMiner software is its ability to provide performance details in an easy to visualize graph for tracking your mining activities. It is available for Windows, Mac OS X, and Linux platforms.

Mining apps

Bitcoin mining apps are also becoming increasingly popular. Programmers and companies have begun to notice the trend in the use of Bitcoin as a digital currency and have moved into the market to meet the growing demand. Below are some of the best Bitcoin mining apps available today. They are grouped into four different categories: Tools, Payments, Wallets, and Games.

TOOLS

1. The ICO App

This Bitcoin mining app provides detailed listings of initial coin offerings. It gives a comprehensive profile of tokens, simultaneously giving direct links to their whitepapers and crowdfunding pages. A particularly intriguing feature of the ICO app is its notification alert feature for token sale opening and closing dates. It also includes a news section and can be downloaded from Google Play Store, free of charge.

2. Coindex

Coindex offers crypto portfolio tracking in an easy to use interface. Some of its main features include candlestick charts, market data, multiple portfolios and market cap listings. It is a must-have for any investor in the crypto space. Irrespective of your level of experience, Coindex is a vital tool that would set you up for success. It can be downloaded from both the Google Play Store and App Store for IOS, free of charge.

3. Blackfolio

Blackfolio is another Bitcoin mining app that is packed with features to keep you well informed about the Bitcoin and cryptocurrency markets. Some noteworthy features of this app include detailed price information and preset notifications for when the price crosses a certain limit. It is the perfect tool for keeping an eye on the cryptocurrency markets and an invaluable resource for trading on them. It can be downloaded from both the Google Play Store and App Store for IOS, free of charge.

34

4. Lawnmower

The lawnmower is a Bitcoin investment app which enables you to earn Bitcoin through the investment of your fiat money. It automatically synchronizes your fiat bank account with your Coinbase account where your Bitcoins are stored and converts your money into Bitcoins. It is a great way to save your money by putting it towards building your Bitcoin earnings. It can be downloaded from both the Google Play Store and App Store for IOS, free of charge.

5. Getgems

Getgems is another Bitcoin mining tool, and this one pays you to text people. Unlike other mining apps that deal with BTC, Getgems deals specifically with GEMZ. It is also a decentralized cryptocurrency, and it is earned via referrals. Usually, you refer someone to the app, and when the person becomes a new participant, you earn 25 GEMZ, which is the equivalent of $0.25. You can transfer the money to Lawnmower via the messaging service within the app. Getgems can be downloaded from both the Google Play Store and App Store for IOS, free of charge.

PAYMENTS

1. BitPay

Bitpay has been renowned for making Bitcoin payments via its website, and now they're extending their "one-touch" Bitcoin payments to mobile devices. They aim to achieve this through their Bitcoin checkout app. It can be downloaded from both the Google Play Store and App Store for IOS.

2. Gliph

Gliph has been described as the ultimate Bitcoin marketplace. It has lots of functions that exceeds being a mere payment app. It allows you to send and receive messages to individuals or within groups. You can also put items on display you have for sale and also purchase items all using your mobile device or via your desktop computer. It is a well-rounded mobile app that aims to revolutionize the cryptocurrency marketplace. It can be downloaded from both the Google Play Store and App Store for IOS.

3. Spare

The Spare app allows you to turn your Bitcoin into cash quickly and conveniently. All you have to do is to request for cash using an ATM. You will receive a barcode which you will take to a local shop near you. The shopkeeper will then scan the code and give you cash in exchange. Spare also works with fiat currency, thus eliminating the need for an ATM. Spare is available for download only on the App Store for IOS.

4. Fold

Fold app is a favorite for retailers. It allows users to make Bitcoin payments for their purchases at stores such as Starbucks, Target, and Whole Foods from the convenience of their mobile devices. Fold app's developers are currently in the process of adding retailers, a move that will revolutionize mobile payments. It will soon be available for download in the various app stores.

WALLETS

Wallets are mining apps that provide a safe and secure location for storing and accessing your Bitcoins from your mobile device. Some of the best Bitcoin wallets include:

1. Xapo

Xapo is the "only fully insured Bitcoin storage solution." It allows you to send and receive Bitcoins in an easy two-step process. It doesn't require payment of any fees, and it can be downloaded on both the Google Play Store and App Store for IOS, free of charge.

2. Circle

Circle is more than just a wallet, it is a Bitcoin exchange app that enables you to store, access, send, receive and convert your Bitcoins using your mobile device. You can create your own QR codes using the app as well.

You can download Circle from both the Google Play Store and App Store for IOS, free of charge.

3. Blockchain

The Blockchain wallet app is arguably the most commonly-used Bitcoin wallet, and it is widely known for its incredible security. The Blockchain wallet is an open source app that allows you to send and receive Bitcoins, view transactions and access up to 22 different currencies. It doesn't end there; Blockchain also allows you to scan paper wallets and browse for Bitcoin merchants that are close to you. It is currently available for download on both the Google Play Store and App Store for IOS, free of charge.

GAMES

Finally, we have the mining games. There are actually some mobile games that can help you earn real Bitcoins. Some of them include:

1. Bitcoin Billionaire

Bitcoin Billionaire is a great mobile game for Bitcoin mining. It simply involves tapping the screen to earn more coins, make upgrades to you mining office and ultimately become a Bitcoin Billionaire! It is currently available for download on both the Google Play Store and App Store for IOS, free of charge.

2. FlapPig

FlapPig was created by BitLanders and follows the same modus operandi as the popular game Flappy Bird. In this game, you help Foo the golden pig fly around and collect Bitcoins while dodging obstacles. You will be rewarded and earn real Bitcoins. It is currently available for download on both the Google Play Store and App Store for IOS, free of charge.

3. Bitcoin Fighter

Bitcoin Fighter is a game with two fighters pitted against each other, where they both have to fight for a price of wagered Bitcoins. The game is still in Beta mode and can either be played via the app or in the tournament from its website. You can download it for free from the Google Play Store.

Electrical costs for mining

Bitcoin mining consumes a lot of electricity, and that costs money. As earlier pointed out, the cost of the mining hardware and the monthly electricity fees are the two most expensive things in any mining operation. When not planned and managed properly, the electrical costs for mining can consume all of your profits.

You need to figure out how many hashes you are getting for every watt of electricity that you consume. This can be done by dividing the hash count by the number of watts. For instance, if you have a 500 GH/sec device which consumes 400 watts of power, it means you're getting 1.25 GH/sec per watt.

Check your electricity bill or use an online electricity price calculator to find out how much it translates to in hard cash. For optimum results, it is recommended that you run a mining operation in a location where you can get the cheapest electricity.

China currently has the highest concentration of Bitcoin miners because of the country's cheap electricity. Chinese pools control approximately 81% of the network hash rate. China is also home to many of the top Bitcoin mining companies including AntPool, F2Pool, BTCC, and BW.

In the US, Washington State has the most mining hardware due to the cheap hydroelectricity located there. Also, in Venezuela, Bitcoin mining has become very profitable because of the crisis and the cheap electricity being enjoyed there.

Other Bitcoin Mining Options

Cloud Mining

Cloud mining provides the option for miners who want to earn Bitcoins without having to manage their own hardware. You simply pay a service provider to mine for you, and you get the rewards. It is a very useful alternative for those who aren't technically minded.

Also, if you live in an area where electricity cost is high, it is a good idea to outsource your mining to areas where electricity costs are cheaper. You use shared processing power run from remote data centers. All you need is a computer for communications, optional local Bitcoin wallets, etc.

There are currently three types of cloud mining available, they are:

1. **Hosted mining:** where you lease a mining machine that is hosted by the provider.

2. **Virtually hosted mining:** where you create a virtual private server and install your own mining software.

3. **Leased hashing power:** this is arguably the most popular method of cloud mining. Here, you lease an amount of hashing power, without having a dedicated physical or virtual computer.

Mining Pools

Mining pools as earlier explained is a collection of miners who work together to reduce the volatility of their returns. It is a strategic approach to mining where multiple miners contribute to the generation of a block and then split the rewards according to each miner's contributed processing power.

The functions of a mining pool revolve around the following activities:

1. Collecting the pool member's hashes
2. Looking for block rewards
3. Recording the amount of work each participant is doing
4. Assigning block rewards in proportion to each participant's hashpower

There are a few things you need to consider when joining a mining pool. First, you need to ensure that you take into account the pool's method of distributing their block reward. Secondly, make sure that you confirm the Pool fees charged for managing the pool. The Pool fees usually range from 0% to 4%, but the standard fee for most mining pools is 1%.

Below is a list of the 10 best and biggest Mining Pools currently in operation:

- AntPool
- BTC.top
- BTC.com
- Bixin
- BTCC
- F2pool
- ViaBTC
- BW Pool
- Bitclub.Network
- Slush

How to set up a Bitcoin mining operation

Setting up a Bitcoin mining operation is quite a complex task and requires investing some time and effort on your part. You may choose to buy a cloud mining contract with Hashflare or Genesis Mining as an alternative, or you could purchase a mining rig.

Once that's done, choose a mining pool to join and make sure that your wallet is also linked and ready to run. If, however, your rig, FGPA or graphics card fails to run, try the following steps:

Step 1: Download the full Bitcoin client. Depending on your download speed, this may take quite a few days.

Step 2: Download some Bitcoin mining software – or the program that controls your mining hardware

Step 3: Join a mining pool

Regarding simplicity, Spondoolies tech is the most user-friendly miner you could begin with. Plug in the SP20 or SP10 into your router and follow the five sets of instructions to get your Bitcoin miner up and running.

Next, you need to choose a means to supply power. Some miners have built-in power supplies, while for others, you will need to purchase external PSU (Power Supply Units). Ensure that the units bought have the necessary power to coincide with that of the mining chips.

Also, make sure that you complete the circuit for the PSU to allow electricity to flow. You can do this by taking the 24 pin connector and attaching a paperclip from the green wire to any black wire. After that, you will have completed the circuit, and the PSU will switch on.

How to Calculate Bitcoin Mining Profits

To calculate your Bitcoin mining profits, you will need to find out your electricity rate. You can find this in your monthly electricity bill. Note that the future profitability of Bitcoin mining cannot be ascertained because of the ever-changing nature of the Difficulty modifier and the BTC price.

Nonetheless, you can still determine your current mining profitability. To being with, you must select a suitable ASIC mining rig. It is advisable that you go for the AntMiner S7 from Bitmain. Compute its specs and cost, including other information such as power cost and pool fees.

You can also use websites like CoinWarz.com which provides a good platform for calculating mining profitability. This site automatically enters the current BTC price, Difficulty and block reward information when performing mining profitability calculations.

Remember to include your default power cost, which can be confirmed from your utility bill, add the Pool fee as well and compare the Pool fees with the reward structure. After you have filled in all the requisite info, click Calculate to generate the profitability result.

Risks and Rewards of Bitcoin Mining

Risks

Possible risks of mining Bitcoins include:

1. Susceptible to high price volatility: This is one of the main risks of Bitcoin mining. The price of the cryptocurrency is not stable, and it usually tends to fluctuate very often. Its price depends on its demand and supply, and the demand keeps increasing daily when there are only 21 million Bitcoins available.

2. Competition with other cryptocurrencies such as Ethereum: Bitcoin's current value caps at 12.5 BTC, with an average block time of 10 minutes. Ethereum's block time, on the other hand, is 12 second. With a faster block time, Ethereum thus confirms its transactions much faster. Ethereum also has over 89 million coins currently unmined, unlike Bitcoin that has

fewer. If Bitcoin reaches its threshold, more investors will move to Ethereum or other cryptocurrencies.

3. The "hard fork" issue: Due to Bitcoin's increasing popularity, it is unable to manage the weight of all the transactions taking place on the network. Its current 1MB block size limit is quite small and is causing delays in its speed of processing payments. This has given rise to the hard fork issue which is the splitting of the network into two – Bitcoin Unlimited (BU) and Segregated Witness (SegWit). Miners and developers are presently at loggerheads about this issue, and it is increasing the uncertainty about the future of the cryptocurrency.

Rewards

Bitcoin mining is a very profitable activity. Aside from the monetary rewards you can earn from it, some of its other rewards include:

1. No interruptions by third-parties
2. Payment ease
3. No taxation
4. Very low transaction fees
5. Faster transactions
6. Completely transparent
7. No tracking

CONCLUSION

We have been able to provide a basic understanding of what Bitcoin mining is all about. The information contained above should be enough to get you started on Bitcoin mining. Some of the top things you should keep in mind, however, before starting your own mining operation include:

1. Make sure that you understand the meaning of all the basic technical terms commonly used in Bitcoin mining.

2. Ensure that you do your own research and understand the fees and reward structure for the mining pool that you want to join before applying.

3. Check the cost of the electricity in your area before setting up a mining operation. Only mine from a location that has cheap electricity.

4. Determine the type of mining hardware you want to use and go for one that you can afford.

5. Be careful of using outdated mining software as it is easier to hack into.

6. Always stay updated with the latest mining apps for Tools, Payments, Wallets, and Games.

7. Use only reputable mining calculators to determine your profits.

8. Be careful of the type of service provider you choose to manage your cloud mining operations. Make sure you do your research before hiring one.

9. Use Spondoolies tech when setting up your mining operation. It is the most user-friendly miner you should begin with.

10. Bitcoin mining comes with possible risks and rewards. Make sure that you understand and are well prepared for them.

9 787002 472080

Printed by Libri Plureos GmbH in Hamburg, Germany